Thank you for buying this Comic Relief book.

You are a complete star for doing so and are already half-way to becoming a fundraising supremo! The idea behind it is to raise as much cash as possible for Comic Relief while having a bit of fun in the kitchen and enjoying some lovely food and company at the same time. What could be better than that?

So, I've come up with an idea. *Funky Cooking* gives you four different themed evenings, each of which has a menu provided, with recipes which you can keep for ever. Whether you're a complete beginner in the kitchen, or you like to be challenged with dishes that are a little bit harder, you'll find something here to get stuck into. The first menu is the easiest and the last one is more involved. All you have to do is pick the evening party that you want to throw and charge your mates/boyfriend/girlfriend/family an entrance fee to attend and enjoy your delicious food and company! Easy as that. To make things a bit more interesting you could even ask them to pay extra for waitress service (and rope in a friend to help with this). Make sure they give a good tip, and donate that too!

If you're still at school, you'll find some recipes on page 29 for food that you can take in and sell to your classmates and teachers to make a bit of extra dosh. Or you can sell them to your workmates. You'll find a sponsorship form on page 30 to help you along. There are recipes for everyone to try, so have a look and see which ones take your fancy. So let's all get cooking and raise cash for Comic Relief.

I bet you're wondering what happens to the money that you make after all this cooking and entertaining. Well, from every single book that is sold, £2.00 goes straight to Comic Relief, which they use to help some of the poorest people here in the UK and in Africa. Have a look at page 32 to see where some of the money will end up. And don't forget to watch the night of Comic Relief on Red Nose Day (14 March 2003), curled up in front of your TV with some lovely tucker.

PS If you're wondering why my hair is looking so strange here, it's not that I've had a change of image – it's because Red Nose Day this year is all about Funky Hairstyles! So make sure you do something outrageous to your hair and wear it like that at your dinner party, or all day long on 14 March.

Lo...

A Beginner's Dinner Party

This is the perfect menu to have a go at making if you're not all that confident in the kitchen. The recipes are easy to follow and the results are amazing. You'll be having a go at all the other menus after you've tried this one out, so get stuck in!

CHICKPEA, LEEK AND PARMESAN SOUP

SERVES 4

2 medium leeks | 1 tablespoon butter | 2 cloves of garlic, peeled and chopped
| 1 handful of fresh thyme, leaves picked | 1 can of chickpeas, drained and rinsed
| 565ml chicken stock | 2 medium potatoes, peeled and chopped | salt
and freshly ground black pepper | extra virgin olive oil | 250g Parmesan cheese

Trim the outside of the leeks back then cut off any coarse green tops and discard them. Cut the leeks in half lengthways and slice the halves into fine shreds. Put the chopped leeks in a colander and rinse thoroughly under running water, removing any dirt. In a large saucepan, gently heat the butter and add the garlic, leeks and thyme leaves. Put the lid on the pot and slowly cook until soft without colouring.

Add the chickpeas to the leeks with the chicken stock and the potatoes. Bring to the boil then simmer gently for half an hour or so or until the potatoes are well cooked. If the soup is too thick, loosen it with a little boiling water.

Break up the chickpeas and pieces of potato to thicken it slightly. Season carefully with salt and freshly ground black pepper, and pour into hot bowls. Top with a splash of olive oil and some grated Parmesan cheese.

SEA BASS BAKED IN A BAG WITH FRESH HERBS AND FENNEL

SERVES 4

1 red onion, peeled and finely sliced | 1 bulb of fennel, finely sliced | 2 plum tomatoes, chopped | 1 clove of garlic, peeled and finely sliced | 4 handfuls of mixed fresh herbs (parsley, basil, fennel, bay) | 2 x 700g sea bass, scaled and gutted | sea salt and freshly ground black pepper | 1 dessertspoon fennel seeds | 3 lemons | 1 small handful of black olives, stoned | extra virgin olive oil

Preheat the oven to 220°C/425°F/gas 7. Tear off 2 pieces of kitchen foil about 5 times as long as each fish, then fold these in half to give you double thickness. In the middle of one half of each piece of foil, sprinkle equal amounts of the red onion, fennel, tomato, garlic and half of the herbs. Season each fish inside and out with sea salt, freshly ground black pepper and the fennel seeds, then stuff with the rest of the herbs – use just one herb or a mixture of your favourites. Place your fish snugly on top of the veg. Squeeze over the juice from 2 of the lemons, then slice the third lemon and lay a few slices on top of each fish. Scatter over the olives and drizzle with olive oil.

For each parcel, fold the foil over the fish and seal the 3 open edges neatly and tightly, being careful not to pierce the foil, as this will let the juices escape. Cook on a baking tray in the preheated oven for 20 minutes. When done, take the puffed-up bags to the table and let your guests pierce them for a bit of theatre. It will smell fantastic! Serve with some simple boiled potatoes.

BRUSCHETTA WITH ROASTED FRUIT

This recipe is so simple. Feel free to use any good seasonal fruit with stones and instead of sourdough you can use use pannetone bread slices to give it a nice twist. It's also well worth making yourself some vanilla sugar once a year.

SERVES 4

12 pieces of fruit (pears, plums, peaches, apricots, nectarines) | 8 tablespoons vanilla sugar | 1 wineglass of brandy | a few sprigs of fresh lemon thyme or rosemary | 4 slices of sourdough bread | 4 large knobs of butter | 1 tub of good vanilla ice cream or crème fraîche

Preheat the oven to 220°C/425°F/gas 7. Cut the fruit in half and remove the stones. Lay the fruit snugly in a heatproof dish, sprinkle with the sugar and pour over the brandy. Lay the herb sprigs on top then cook in the preheated oven for about 15 minutes, until soft.

Lightly toast the slices of sourdough and butter well. Pile the warm fruit on top and drizzle with any juices from the tray. Serve with a good scoop of vanilla ice cream or crème fraîche.

A Curry with Your Mates!

Everyone loves a good curry, and your mates are bound to love you even more if you serve them these fragrant dishes. Get some lovely chutneys and pickles in, with some naan bread and poppadums, and you'll be set for a great evening. Beer is always best with a curry, but I've included a non-alcoholic drink here as an alternative.

MANGO LASSI

This Indian drink is like a mango milkshake and is delicious. You can also make it using banana instead of mango – give both a try. In India the sugar is sometimes replaced by salt to make it savoury.

SERVES 4

255ml plain yoghurt | 130ml milk | 130ml canned mango pulp or 200g fresh mango, stoned and sliced | 4 teaspoons sugar, to taste

Put all the ingredients into a blender and blend for 2 minutes, then pour into individual glasses and serve. The lassi can be kept refrigerated for up to 24 hours.

CAULIFLOWER, PEA AND POTATO BHAJI

This makes a great veggie snack stuffed in some grilled pitta bread with a bit of fresh mint and seasoned yoghurt.

SERVES 4

a bunch of fresh coriander | 4 medium potatoes, peeled and diced | 1 cauliflower, broken into florets | a pinch of black mustard seeds | $^1/_2$ teaspoon of cumin seeds | $^1/_2$ teaspoon of fennel seeds | $^1/_2$ teaspoon of fenugreek seeds | $^1/_2$ teaspoon of coriander seeds | salt and freshly ground black pepper | 1 tablespoon butter | 1 onion, peeled and finely sliced | a pinch of turmeric | a handful of frozen peas | 4 ripe tomatoes, roughly chopped | 1 fresh red chilli, thinly sliced

Preheat the oven to 220°C/425°F/gas 7. Remove the stalks from the coriander and chop finely. Put these to one side then chop the leaves. Now boil the potatoes and cauliflower for 10 minutes.

Bash all the whole spices to a powder with a teaspoon of salt, using a pestle and mortar. Melt the butter in a pan and fry the onion gently for 5 minutes with the coriander stalks until soft. Add the spice mixture and the turmeric and fry gently for another minute. Drain the potatoes and cauliflower and add to the pan with the peas and chopped tomato. Stir everything together then season to taste. Place in a baking dish and cook in the oven for about 15–20 minutes until golden. When serving, sprinkle with the chopped coriander leaves and chilli.

HOT CHICKEN CURRY WITH CHILLI AND GREEN HERBS

This curry also works well with lamb, beef, white fish or just a selection of vegetables.

SERVES 4

1 teaspoon turmeric | juice of 2 limes | salt and freshly ground black pepper | sunflower oil | 5 cloves of garlic | 10cm fresh ginger | 6 chicken legs, skinned and cut into thighs and drumsticks | 1 tablespoon butter | 2 red onions, peeled and finely sliced | 350ml natural yoghurt | a bunch of fresh coriander | a bunch of fresh dill | a small bunch of fresh mint | 4 fresh green chillies

In a big bowl, combine the turmeric, the lime juice, a few pinches of salt and a splash of sunflower oil. Peel the garlic and ginger, chop them roughly, then pound them to a paste using a pestle and mortar or food processor. Add to the bowl, with the chicken pieces, stir well, and leave to marinate for an hour or so.

Heat a large wide pot big enough to hold all the chicken pieces. Add a splash of sunflower oil and the butter, then put in the onions and cook gently over a low heat until soft. Add the chicken pieces to the pan and cook for another 10 minutes or so, making sure that nothing gets too dark and starts to burn. Pour in the yoghurt and give everything a good stir. Bring to a simmer and cook very gently for 10 to 20 minutes until the chicken is cooked and tender.

Meanwhile, chop the green herbs and the chillies roughly. You can take the seeds out of the chillies if you don't want things to get too spicy! Put the herbs and chillies into a blender with 150ml of warm water and blend until you have what looks like a bright green smoothie. Stir it into the cooked chicken and heat through gently. Taste and season with salt and freshly ground black pepper before serving with some basmati rice, lots of ice cold lassi and Indian beer!

If you've got your eye on that special someone then this is the menu to cook for them. Not only will it make them sit up and take notice of your amazing cooking skills, but it's guaranteed to succeed in making them notice you too!

PENNE CARBONARA

SERVES 2

300g dried penne pasta | salt and freshly ground black pepper | 5 slices of pancetta or smoky bacon | olive oil | 2 large organic egg yolks | 50ml double cream | 75g Parmesan cheese, grated

Cook the penne in salted boiling water until al dente. Fry the pancetta in a little oil until crispy and then put to one side. In a bowl, whip up the egg yolks, cream and half the Parmesan. When the pasta is cooked, drain it and immediately toss it with the warm, crispy pancetta and the egg mixture. Many carbonaras are over-cooked like scrambled eggs – if you add the penne immediately, the residual heat is enough to cook the eggs and for the sauce to stay smooth and silky. Season well, using plenty of freshly ground black pepper, and add extra Parmesan to taste.

CHICKEN WITH BASIL BUTTER AND PANCETTA

You can adjust this recipe to use pork chops, a rack of lamb or even a whole fish.

SERVES 2

600g potatoes, peeled and cut into 1cm slices | salt and freshly ground black pepper | olive oil | a bunch of fresh basil | 50g softened butter | 2 skinless chicken breasts | 12 thin slices of pancetta | 1 large handful of cherry tomatoes | a handful of stoned black olives | a small bunch of rocket | juice of ½ a lemon | 4 tablespoons extra virgin olive oil

Preheat the oven to 220°C/425°F/gas 7. Parboil the potatoes in salted water then drain and let them steam dry until cool. Toss with a little oil and seasoning. Spread the slices out evenly on a baking tray and bake in the oven for about 10 minutes.

Chop the basil leaves roughly and pound them in a pestle and mortar with a little salt until you have a bright green paste. Add a little butter and pound again. Gradually add the rest of the butter, mixing it in well each time.

Turn your first chicken breast over, fold back the small fillet that you find underneath, and cut a long shallow slash into the main breast muscle. Spoon a couple of teaspoons of your basil butter into this incision and fold the small fillet back into its original position to keep the butter in place. Repeat with the other chicken breast.

Tear a sheet of baking parchment into 2 rough squares and lay 6 pancetta slices, slightly overlapping, on each square. Lay a chicken breast upside down on each of the squares and use the paper to help you wrap the breasts neatly in the pancetta. Your chicken is now ready to roast!

Cut the cherry tomatoes in half and mix them with the olives and another glug of oil. When the potatoes are nearly cooked, throw the olives and tomatoes over them and place the wrapped chicken breasts on top. Put back in the oven for about 15 to 20 minutes, or until the chicken and potatoes are cooked and crispy. Mix the lemon juice with the extra virgin olive oil, dress the rocket and serve with the chicken.

TROPICAL FRUIT JELLY

SERVES 2, WITH ENOUGH FOR SECONDS!

1 ripe mango, peeled and thinly sliced | 100g lychees, peeled and thinly sliced | 2 leaves of gelatine | 70ml elderflower cordial | 2 heaped tablespoons caster sugar | 200ml prosecco (sparkling Italian wine), chilled | 1 vanilla pod | 50g icing sugar | 200ml double cream | 1 bunch mint

First of all, decide whether you want to make one big jelly or small individual ones. If you are making a big one, it's a good idea to line the container with clingfilm first. Mix your mango and lychee slices together then place into your mould or moulds and put in the fridge to chill.

Put your gelatine leaves into a bowl with a little cold water to soak for a minute, then drain and add the gelatine back to the bowl with the elderflower cordial. Rest this bowl above a pan of water on a medium heat and stir constantly until the gelatine and cordial become a syrup. At this point you can add your sugar. Stir until dissolved, then remove the bowl from the heat and let it sit at room temperature for a minute or so.

Take your chilled fruit and prosecco out of the fridge. The idea here is that because the fruit, moulds and prosecco are all chilled, the bubbles will stay in the jelly when it sets and will fizz in your mouth when you eat it – beautiful! Pour the prosecco into your cordial mix, and then pour this over your fruit. Some of the fruit might rise to the top so use your finger to push it down into the jelly mix. You want to make sure that it's completely covered – this will seal it and will ensure it keeps well in the fridge. Put back into the fridge for an hour to set.

When you are ready to serve, slit the vanilla pod lengthways and scrape out the little black seeds into a bowl. Add the icing sugar and cream and then whip together with a whisk until just stiff. Serve with the jelly and a sprig of mint. Lovely!

A Menu to Impress

A really colourful, professional-looking dinner. Invite your family, your mother-in-law or your boss round but don't forget to make them pay up for the privilege of tasting your cooking! They won't fail to be impressed...

ROAST SQUASH, SAGE, CHESTNUT AND PANCETTA RISOTTO

SERVES 6

1 butternut squash | 1 level tablespoon coriander seeds | 2 small dried chillies | sea salt and freshly ground black pepper | olive oil | 1.1 litres chicken or vegetable stock | 1 knob of butter | 1 large onion, peeled and finely chopped | 2 cloves of garlic, peeled and finely chopped | 1/2 a head of celery, finely chopped | 400g risotto rice | 2 wineglasses of dry white vermouth or dry white wine | 12 slices of pancetta or dry-cured smoky bacon | 100g chestnuts (vac-packed are fine) | a bunch of fresh sage, leaves picked | 70g butter | 115g freshly grated Parmesan cheese | 6 heaped tablespoons mascarpone cheese

Preheat your oven to 190°C/375°F/gas 5. Carefully cut your butternut squash in half and scoop out the seeds. Put these to one side. Cut the squash lengthways into 0.5cm slices and put in a large bowl. Bash up your coriander seeds and chillies with a pinch of salt and pepper, using a pestle and mortar. Dust this over your squash with a tablespoon of olive oil. Toss around until completely coated. Line the pieces of squash up snugly in a roasting tray and bake for around 30 minutes, until soft to the touch.

While the squash is baking, heat the stock. In a separate pan heat 2 tablespoons of olive oil with the knob of butter, add the onion, garlic and celery, and fry very slowly for about 15 minutes without colouring. When the vegetables have softened, add the rice and turn up the heat. It will begin to fry, so keep stirring it. After a minute it will look slightly translucent. Add the vermouth or wine and keep stirring – it will smell fantastic.

Once the vermouth or wine has cooked into the rice, add your first ladle of hot stock and a good pinch of salt. Turn down the heat to a simmer so the rice doesn't cook too quickly on the outside. Keep adding ladlefuls of stock, stirring and massaging the creamy starch out of the rice, allowing each ladleful to be absorbed before adding the next. This will take around 15 minutes. Carry on adding stock until the rice is soft but with a slight bite. If you run out of stock before the rice is cooked, add some boiling water. Check for seasoning.

When the squash is cooked, remove it from the oven and lay your slices of pancetta over it. In a small bowl, mix the squash seeds, chestnuts and sage leaves with a little olive oil, salt and pepper. Sprinkle over the squash and pancetta and put back in the oven for 5 to 10 minutes until the pancetta is crisp. Once the squash has cooled down a little, shake off the pancetta and chestnuts and finely chop the squash. Add this to the risotto and mix together.

Remove the risotto from the heat and add the 70g butter and Parmesan. Stir well, then place a lid on the pan and allow to sit for 2 minutes. Season to taste and serve with the pancetta, chestnuts, sage leaves and squash seeds sprinkled over the top and a big dollop of mascarpone cheese on the side.

ROASTED ROYAL BREAM

Try serving this with some lovely salsa verde. You can also use different fish, depending on what looks good.

SERVES 4

olive oil | 4 x 225g bream fillets | 1 handful of mixed fresh herbs (green or purple basil, flat-leaf parsley, thyme), roughly chopped | 1kg potatoes, scrubbed | 2 cloves of garlic, peeled and finely chopped | salt and freshly ground black pepper | 3 knobs of butter | 325g mixed, preferably wild, mushrooms, torn | juice of 1 lemon | 12 baby leeks, blanched

Preheat the oven to 220°C/350°F/gas 4. Put a bit of greaseproof paper on the bottom of a baking tray and rub it with olive oil. Slash the fish fillets about half-way down and stuff the slashes with the herbs. Slice the potatoes lengthways, just under 1cm thick. Dry them with kitchen paper, then put them into a large bowl and very lightly coat them in olive oil. Mix in half of your garlic, season with salt and freshly ground black pepper, then lay the potatoes out in one layer on your baking tray and cook in the preheated oven for around 20 minutes until just tender.

Put the rest of the garlic into a pan with 2 good knobs of butter and a lug of olive oil. Fry your mixed mushrooms and season until tasty. If water comes out of them just continue cooking until it evaporates. Take the pan off the heat, squeeze in the lemon juice and stir in another knob of butter. Now scatter the mushrooms and blanched leeks over the potatoes and rub them on top, underneath, all over. Place your bream fillets on top, and bake in the preheated oven for 12–15 minutes, depending on the thickness of your fish.

When the fish is done, remove the tray from the oven, put some kitchen foil over the top and let it sit for about 5 minutes, during which time all the lovely juices will run out into the potatoes. Serve drizzled with a little extra virgin olive oil.

VENEZUELAN CHOCOLATE POTS

I call these 'Venezuelan' as I tried making them with the most delicious Venezuelan chocolate called El Rey – try to get hold of some or just use the best chocolate you can find.

SERVES 4

a large knob of butter, softened | 250g caster sugar | 50g each of hazelnuts and almonds, shelled | 140g unsalted butter | 150g best-quality cooking chocolate (70% cocoa solids) | 8 tablespoons cocoa powder, sifted | a small pinch of salt | 4 eggs | 3 tablespoons golden syrup | 7 medium heaped tablespoons sour cream or crème fraîche | a good glug of Vin Santo | $^1/_2$ an orange, zested

Rub the softened butter around the inside of 4 little coffee cups. Put 50g sugar in a pan and drizzle enough water over to dissolve the sugar. Stir together. Leave on the heat until the mixture reaches a caramel colour. Add the nuts and pour on to a greased plate or tray to cool. Break the caramel into pieces and blitz in a Magimix food processor to make your praline powder. Sprinkle this into your buttered cups to coat the insides.

Preheat the oven to 150°C/300°F/gas 2. Place the unsalted butter, chocolate, cocoa powder and salt in a bowl over a pan of simmering water and allow to melt slowly, stirring occasionally until well mixed. In a separate bowl beat the eggs and sugar together until light and well creamed, and then add the golden syrup and 3 tablespoons of sour cream or crème fraîche. Stir your chocolate mix into your egg mix, scraping all the chocolate out with a spatula. Once you've mixed it well, pour it into the prepared coffee cups. Stand the cups in a large roasting tin and pour hot water into the tin to come half-way up the cups. Carefully place in the preheated oven and cook for about 20 minutes. During cooking a beautiful crust will form on top.

Remove from the oven and allow to cool. Serve with the remaining sour cream or crème fraîche mixed with Vin Santo and orange zest.

Kids' Stuff

Here are some funky little recipes which you can take into school (or work!) to sell to your mates. They are dead easy to make, so get stuck in and raise some extra money for Comic Relief. Put your own price on the portions and take it from there. You'll also find a sponsorship form on page 30 so you can take orders, for a price!

CHOCOLATE CHIP COOKIES

MAKES ABOUT 20

350g chocolate | 60g butter | 4 eggs | 135g caster sugar | 60g flour
| 1 dessertspoon baking powder | 300g chocolate chips

Melt the chocolate and butter in a small pan and set aside to cool. Whisk the
eggs and sugar in a bowl until pale and thick. Gently fold in the flour, the
baking powder and the cooled chocolate mixture. Add the chocolate chips
and continue to fold everything together. Chill in the fridge until hard.

Preheat the oven to 180°C/350°F/gas 4. Spoon walnut-size pieces of the
dough on to a baking tray covered with greaseproof paper. Bake for 5 minutes, then remove from the oven and leave to cool on the tray.

PS If you like almonds then these cookies are great with some added. Just
use 100g and roughly chop them and add with the chocolate chips.

CHOCOLATE FRIDGE CAKE

MAKES ABOUT 10 SLICES

200g Digestive biscuits | 100g pecan nuts, shelled | 100g pistachio
nuts, shelled | 10 glacé cherries | 150g butter | 1 tablespoon golden syrup
| 1 tablespoon sugar | 200g good-quality chocolate

Break the biscuits into small pieces directly into a large bowl. Then add the
pecans, pistachios and cherries. Put the rest of the ingredients into a sec-
ond heatproof bowl and either put this over a pan of simmering water or into
a microwave oven until melted.

Mix the contents of both bowls together and get yourself a container
which will act as your mould. To help with turning out, line the container
with clingfilm, leaving plenty of extra film at the edges to fold over the top.
Now spoon the mixture into the container. Put into the fridge to firm up,
then turn out, removing the clingfilm, and cut into chunky slices. This cake
can be kept in an airtight container and actually improves after a couple of
days.

PS If you're allergic to nuts then simply leave them out of the recipe.

the **sponsorship** form

- I want to get stuck in like Jamie, and am cooking up a storm for Comic Relief.
- I am happy to say that you – yes you! – have been specially selected to be the proud owner of some of my hair-raisingly lip-smacking good food.
- I have been working very hard, mixing and chopping and everything. All you need to do is fork out some cash in exchange for some really tasty grub. Then I will give the cash to Comic Relief. Are you getting a good deal or what?

A Word from the Chancellor of the Exchequer:
'If you pay tax and you tick the Gift Aid box on this sheet the government will be giving Comic Relief 28% on top of your donation. It won't cost you a penny.'

giftaid it

Very important box
Please tick if you would
like Comic Relief to reclaim
the tax on your donation
Costs you nothing, earns us lots

Name	Full address including postcode (don't forget to fill this bit in, otherwise we can't claim Gift Aid)	Total sponsored	Total received	
		£	£	

Please return this form and all money raised to:
Red Nose Day 2003, Ernst and Young, PO Box 678, London EC4A 1NT.

Total raised £ [   ]

The official bit you fill in when you've collected all the cash!

Name _____

Address _____

Postcode _____ Telephone _____

Signed _____ Parent/guardian if under 18

Total amount enclosed _____

RND03
THE BIG HAIR DO

Comic Relief,
registered charity 32656

From time to time, we would like to send you further information relating to Comic Relief. If you would like to receive such information, please tick this box. ☐

Have fun, but be careful when you cook. Please make sure that all chicken and meat is properly cooked – you don't want to give your friends and family upset tummies.

Ask permission from an adult if you want to use their kitchen. And make sure you clean up afterwards so you don't get nagged for making a mess.

If you are under 16, please don't collect sponsorship money by yourself, or ask any strangers for donations, or make door-to-door collections.

Ready to start getting some publicity? Why not send your local paper a press release about what you are doing, and a photo of you cooking? Why not put on a red nose or Comic Relief T-shirt for the photo? You must remember to put the following sentence on all publicity material: Comic Relief, registered charity 326568.

You are now officially a Comic Relief cooking star. Collect your cash, pay it in at any bank or building society, or post it to **Red Nose Day 2003, Ernst and Young, PO Box 678, London EC4A 1NT.** Please make cheques/postal orders payable to 'Red Nose Day 2003 Cooking'. Please do not send cash through the post. And remember, you can make your donation rise with Gift Aid. See opposite for more information.

To order your Red Nose Day 2003 fundraising kit, call 09065 500 500 or text the word "KIT" followed by your name, address and postcode to 81190. Ordering will cost £1.50 (plus your usual text charge) which covers printing, postage and packaging.

Red Nose Day 2003 donation line: 08457 910 910

www.rednoseday.com

WHERE DOES YOUR MONEY GO?

Money raised on Red Nose Day reaches people across the UK and Africa. From people living and working on the streets of Addis Ababa in Ethiopia, to women fleeing domestic violence in Cardiff, Comic Relief is supporting projects working with poor, vulnerable and disadvantaged people who need help to change their lives. Here are a couple of examples of projects that have benefited from Comic Relief cash:

HOMELESS INTERNATIONAL

Like any other developing country, Kenya has been experiencing rapid urbanization – the urban population is now estimated at over 15 million and is increasing steadily. As a result, many people are living in slum settlements, which are not officially recognized, and are often kicked off their land. It is estimated that 60% of Nairobi's residents are slum dwellers.

Over the past 5 years, Comic Relief has given Homeless International more than £500,000 for their work in Kenya, Uganda, South Africa, Zimbabwe and Tanzania. The grants are helping people living in slums by giving them loans to buy land where they can build safe and secure homes and start to rebuild their lives.

CHALLENGE FOR YOUTH

Some young people have troubled home lives. Some young people get into difficulties with alcohol or drugs. Some young people find they don't have anyone they really trust to confide in – they don't have the opportunity to talk through things that might be troubling them. This can leave them feeling isolated and unsupported, and often makes it really tough for them to feel like they belong to a community.

Challenge for Youth (CFY) brings positive change to the lives of young men who've had a tough time. They're no angels and many have been on the wrong side of the law, but without support it's pretty likely they'll offend again. By working with these young men, CFY aims to develop their self-esteem and reduce the likelihood of their re-offending. £74,240 of Comic Relief cash is helping Challenge for Youth reach out to young men who often don't get the support they really, really need.